✝ THIRSTING FOR GOD

Prayers from a Monastery

By the Monks of Saint Meinrad Archabbey

Edited by Br. Francis de Sales Wagner, O.S.B.

Path of Life Publications
Spiritual Food for the Christian Journey from Abbey Press

Photographs courtesy of Saint Meinrad Archabbey

Cover photo courtesy of Br. Francis de Sales Wagner, O.S.B.
Cover and book design by Mary E. Bolin

Scripture quotations from New Revised Standard Version

ISBN 978-0-87029-460-0
Library of Congress 2011907768

Published by Abbey Press
1 Hill Drive • St. Meinrad, IN 47577
Printed by Abbey Press in the United States of America

Contents

As a deer longs for flowing streams,
so my soul longs for you, O God.
My soul thirsts for God,
for the living God.
When shall I come and behold
the face of God?

Psalm 42:1-2

PREFACE

In his *Rule* for monks, St. Benedict stresses that the first concern for the new-comer to the monastery is whether he "truly seeks God" (*Rule* 58:7). Proficiency in prayer, perfection in virtue, and position in life are not the standards by which one is judged. What really matters is that the novice truly *seeks* God, and demonstrates that authentic search in his manner of life.

The same can be said of all Christians. No matter who we are, what we do, or how well we do it, as God's children we are called to be one with our Creator—and leading us is Christ, who is the Way, the Truth, and the Life. With Christ we cry out with the Psalmist:

> *O God, you are my God, I seek you,*
>   *my soul thirsts for you;*
> *my flesh faints for you,*
>   *as in a dry and weary land where there is no water.*
> **— Psalm 63:1**

This seeking—this *thirsting*, as the Psalmist so vividly illustrates it—is precisely what is meant by Christian prayer and union with God, regardless of the many ways in which it is expressed. For this reason, just before he died on the cross and handed over his spirit, Jesus says aloud: "I thirst" (John 19:28). It is one of the most profound ways in which Jesus demonstrates his solidarity with humanity in leading us to God.

In this way, water becomes an apt metaphor for prayer, for the spiritual life—and not just any water, but *living* water. Our prayer—the basis of our faith—must be alive and flowing, like a fountain or river. This is why baptismal fonts are filled with moving water, and why Baptism is fundamental to the Christian faith. It is where our lifelong journey toward God begins, and it is through the waters of baptism that we both die and rise with Christ to "walk in newness of life" (Romans 6:4). It is how we as Christians respond to Jesus' universal invitation to "Let anyone who is thirsty come to me, and let the one who believes in me drink" (John 7:37-38).

So, in thirsting for God, we join in prayer as the Body of Christ. Through this living fountain, as it were, the Holy Spirit pours out the faith that overflows into the hearts of one another. Together, with one voice, we pray with and *as* Christ: "I thirst. God, my soul thirsts for you."

The monks of Saint Meinrad Archabbey, like other men and women who have followed the *Rule of St. Benedict* for centuries, dedicate their lives to prayer, work, and community life based on the Gospel and steeped in all of Scripture. Whether chanting the Psalms together, privately and prayerfully reading Scripture, or simply soaking in the resounding silence of God's Word, the monks strive to listen for and respond to the voice of the Lord in the daily rhythm of their lives. They thirst for God, and with Christians everywhere, lift up their hands, call on God's name, and say, "Lord, teach us to pray" (Luke 11:1).

Thirsting for God: Prayers from a Monastery offers a sip from the deep well of contemplation available to us all. The prayers, poems, and reflections shared in this small volume represent the fruit of a significant number of monastic lives—young and old alike—rooted in God's Word and watered by the Spirit. It is not a prayer manual, but rather a limited expression of the many ways in which we seek and thirst for God—whether inside or outside the monastery.

The meditation of 20 monks of varying ages is represented here. Each entry is accompanied by the name of the author and his date of monastic profession as a Benedictine monk of Saint Meinrad Archabbey. These works are not prayer instructions but *prayer*, pure and simple. Some are short and straightforward; others are more poetic, and a few could be termed as reflections. Since the Word of God is so central to the life of a monk, the prayers have been organized according to various aspects of the Christian faith under corresponding chapter headings based on actual Scripture passages and accompanied by a relevant quote from the Bible. The accompanying photographs were all taken on the "Holy Hill"—the grounds of Saint Meinrad Archabbey.

I am grateful to all my confreres in the monastery who have helped in putting this book together—and in so many other ways. Special thanks are due to Fr. Simeon Daly, O.S.B., who offers some thoughts on prayer in the *Introduction*, and Fr. Rupert Ostdick, O.S.B., who submitted a lovely piece (*Reconciliation*) which he penned 60 years ago for a seminary class and specifically retrieved for this project. Between them, Fr. Simeon and Fr. Rupert have been thirsting for God in the monastic way of life for 134 years!

A special note of gratitude also goes to Fr. Harry Hagan, O.S.B., who was my novice-master and is simply a fine human being. He has submitted several very fine pieces. A word of thanks as well to my good friend Br. Mauritius Honegger, O.S.B., a monk of Einsiedeln, our mother abbey in Switzerland, who contributed a prayer for this book while studying here at Saint Meinrad. Thanks to all who submitted some very thoughtful and inspiring pieces for this book, which would otherwise not have been possible.

I would also like to express my appreciation for my co-workers at the Abbey Press who helped with this book, especially Mary Bolin, who does such a fine job as a designer, and Publisher Linus Mundy, who has provided more guidance and support than I can possibly mention. Many thanks as well to the Saint Meinrad Archabbey Development Office—particularly Mike Ziemianski and John Farless —for supporting and assisting this project.

Hopefully, the pages that follow will reveal that our yearning for God in the monastery is not so different from that of any other Christian who genuinely seeks God. Truly, our combined thirst for God reveals a cup that overflows. Let us drink from the never-ending fountain provided by Christ!

Br. Francis de Sales Wagner, O.S.B.
May 2011

Br. Francis, a former newspaper reporter and editor, and a native of Findlay, Ohio, came to Saint Meinrad Archabbey in 2006. He professed his solemn and perpetual vows as a monk of Saint Meinrad in January 2011. He writes and edits for Path of Life Publications *at Abbey Press, studies in the School of Theology, and serves as a conference presenter for the Benedictine Oblate program.*

Introduction

We want to know how to pray. Browse any bookstore spirituality aisle or its online equivalent, and dozens of fairly recent titles on the subject provide us with ample evidence of a sustained interest in prayer in all its forms. Many people, it seems, continue to ask the same question that Jesus' disciples asked: "Lord, teach us to pray" (Luke 11:1).

Surely, most of this interest and concern is genuine. At times, however, I am disconcerted. Are we so caught up in talking about prayer, looking for new methods and signs, that we never come to grips with actually praying? We gather information, probe the esoteric, list obstacles, and distinguish types and techniques. Are we more like art collectors than artists? We become authorities on prayer, its nature and divisions, its history in the church and in society, but do we try to *be* artists?

Some artists, it is true, have unusual perception and gifts, and are able to create works of beauty without much effort. However, most of them become the artists they are through hard work—studying, practicing, and spending long and tedious hours perfecting their craft. I am suggesting that we become prayer artists and not hobbyists, which means we must be willing to work at "learning to pray." This learning process continues to our dying day.

Fundamental to this effort is the commitment to establishing and maintaining a deep, warm, and loving relationship with God. This may be where the basic problem lies. As technology has obscured much of life's mystery, one distorted image—that of a manipulating God constantly arranging the pattern of world events—has yielded to its extreme opposite—a vague concept of a God who is totally removed from us.

It is precisely here that our faith must accept the wholly *Other*, the transcendent, incomprehensible Being whose ways are unsearchable—and yet who also sent his Son to redeem us and teach us to think of him as a loving Father. No matter where we may be in terms of closeness to God, we can all pray with the man in the Gospel: "Lord, help my unbelief" (Mark 9:24). This is a prayer that can be said honestly and still confront the heart of the matter. When we do this we *are* praying. Faith is presupposed in prayer, but it is Christian to pray for a deeper faith.

Placing a value on prayer also means setting aside specific times for it. It means prioritizing our responsibilities, and planning prayer into our day. Simply committing to a specific time for prayer communicates to God and to ourselves that we feel it is important. There is no substitute for this. However prayerfully we may do other things, the importance—and necessity—of this specific time for daily prayer cannot be underestimated. As former Saint Meinrad Archabbey monk Fr. Hilary Ottensmeyer said, "Until you are convinced that prayer is the best use of your time, you will not find time for prayer."

Jesus also tells us to avoid using many words when we pray (Matthew 6:7). We are to place ourselves quietly in God's presence; then, in language that comes "naturally," make our prayer known. There are some basic attitudes that should, at least at times, be reflected in this prayer. First of all, there needs to be the recognition that we are creatures and are dependent on our Creator. We need to have an attitude of reverent awe before God—a recognition that God is worthy of praise and thanks, and that is translated into words. After a time, words are not necessary. The words are not to "tame" God, who knows us better than we know ourselves. Rather, they are the means by which we put *ourselves* in the presence of the God who is always present to us, and remind *ourselves* of God's bounteous goodness, kindness, and providence. As crazy and mixed up as our world is, who of us does not have much to be grateful for?

It is also important to note that prayer should normally be associated with reading. Thought starters are prayer starters, so reading is the launch pad of prayer. Off the printed page, the heart soars. Prayer usually starts with "data." Information from the news, from the events and circumstances of our daily lives, and from reading—especially Sacred Scripture—leads to formulating our intentions in words. Then, when we have said our piece, silence should reign. It is a silence that stems from "reading" and responding to the presence of the Word made flesh. It is in these moments of silence that God reads our hearts and speaks to us.

Yes, prayer can be difficult, especially at the beginning, and it requires a lifetime commitment. But we are not alone; the Spirit of the Lord comes to us where we are and draws us forward (cf. Romans 8:26). This gives zest to a life of prayer. Our perspective on life is always changing. One only has to consider how passages of Scripture can strike us differently at different times in our lives. Words and phrases can take on special meaning depending on where we are at the moment. The same few words may deepen our awareness of our sinfulness at one time and deepen our hope in God's mercy at another. This is the Spirit at work, coming to meet us where we are and drawing us more fully toward Christ.

I have mentioned the man who prayed for faith in the Gospel of Mark. Two other passages come to mind. One is the scene where the blind man asks Jesus, "Lord, that I may see again" (Luke 18:35-43). The other is Jesus' healing of the deaf man: "Ephphatha! Be opened" (Mark 7:31-37). In literal terms, both incidents relate a physical healing as Jesus responds to the particular needs of an individual. However, much more is at stake. Signified in these physical healings is Jesus' healing of the soul through imparting the divine gift of faith. So, wherever we may feel we are in terms of our relationship with God, we can pray for spiritual healing or enrichment:

> *Lord, that I may see; that I may hear and understand. Help me to see beneath the surface of things. Help me to hear you and to understand what you have to say in the events of my life, in the people with whom I deal. Open my mind and heart to whatever it is you are saying to me in these moments of my life. Remove the scales from my eyes; I want to see!*

All creation speaks of God's glory. There are numerous historical events in which God has revealed hidden purposes. When we really believe that our provident Father sustains all things, we rightly pray that he may reveal to us the meaning of any moment in our lives. We can ask with confidence for insight into how we might grow in that moment to a deeper awareness of God so that we may respond with our entire lives to the praise of his glory.

As a librarian, I am well aware of shelf after shelf filled with books on prayer. What I have offered here can only be a sketchy personal reflection. The hope, however, is that some small drop of wisdom here will help deepen your thirst in "learning how to pray." Anyone who is willing to set aside even 10 to 15 minutes a day to rest in God's presence as I have suggested can reasonably hope to gain a clearer understanding of who they are and where they are going in the light of Christ. May you drink in God's abiding peace and joy in abundance.

— Fr. Simeon Daly, O.S.B. (1944)

Fr. Simeon, a native of Michigan, made his solemn vows as a monk of Saint Meinrad Archabbey in 1947 and was ordained to the priesthood in 1948. He was the Archabbey librarian for 49 years. Semi-retired, he does some part-time work for the Archabbey's Development Office, and is the author of the book Finding Grace in the Moment: Stories and Other Musings of an Aged Monk.

ORA

Lord, Teach Us to Pray

Seeking God

Jesus was praying in a certain place,
and after he had finished,
one of his disciples said to him,
"Lord, teach us to pray,
as John taught his disciples."
He said to them, "When you pray, say:
Father, hallowed be your name.
Your kingdom come.
Give us each day our daily bread.
And forgive us our sins,
for we ourselves forgive everyone indebted to us.
And do not bring us to the time of trial."

— Luke 11:1-4

Prayer for the Ability to Pray

Lord Jesus, that disciple St. Luke mentions
has it right when he approaches you and says,
"Lord, teach us to pray…" The simple fact of
our life with you is that we need help to pray.
You obviously understand this because you
answer that disciple with those wondrous
words, "When you pray, say:
'Father, hallowed be thy name. Thy kingdom
come! Give us this day our daily bread,
and forgive us our sins, for we also forgive
everyone who is indebted to us.'"

Lord, I pray you help me to learn and live
this lesson. Amen.

— **Fr. Rupert Ostdick, O.S.B. (1944)**

Teach Us, Lord

Teach us, Lord, what you would say.
Let us pray the prayer you pray.
Let us speak the word you speak.
Help us seek what you would seek.

Show us, Lord, the worlds you know.
Let us go where you would go.
May we see the things you see.
Set us free as you are free.

Let us feel the love you feel.
Let us heal the hurt you heal.
Hold us true to what you hold.
Make us bold as you are bold.

Let us sing the song you sing.
Let us bring the joy you bring.
Let us live as you would live.
Let us give the life you give.

— **Fr. Harry Hagan, O.S.B. (1972)**

Before *Lectio*

Help me, Lord,
as I read your Word,
to hear your voice and understand
what you are saying to me.
Help me meditate on your Word
now and throughout the day,
applying it to all events and circumstances
so that they all become one with your will.

— **Br. Francis de Sales Wagner, O.S.B. (2008)**

Awake, My Soul

Beginning a New Day

Awake, my soul!
Awake, O harp and lyre!
I will awake the dawn.
I will give thanks to you,
O Lord, among the peoples,
and I will sing praises
to you among the nations.
For your steadfast love
is higher than the heavens,
and your faithfulness
reaches to the clouds.

— Psalm 108:1-4

A Prayer for the Morning

Lord God, so far today I have not
been angry, jealous, impatient, lazy,
or gossipy. But I still need your help
because in a minute, I have to get out
of bed.
— **Fr. Joseph Cox, O.S.B. (1998)**

Beginning Again

Dear Lord, I thank you for bringing me to the beginning of a new day. I thank you for the blessings of yesterday, and I ask you to please help me to accept the blessings of this new day in whatever form they may come to me. Grant that I may serve you this day in my prayer and work with attention, reverence, and devotion. Embrace with your love all those whom you will call home to yourself this day, and be for those who will mourn their passing a source of consolation and peace. Amen.

— Fr. Pius Klein, O.S.B. (1959)

Gift of a New Day

I thank you, Lord, for the gift of this
new day, and for bringing me safely
to its beginning.

I thank you for the gift of sleep
during the night.

Grant me the grace I need this day
to walk in your love and your truth.

Above all, Lord, give me the gift of
a joyful heart that in all things I may
see your hand at work and give
myself over to what you want of me
this day.

In Jesus' name I pray. Amen.

— **Archabbot Justin DuVall, O.S.B. (1974)**

Consider Your Call

Choosing the Right Path

Consider your own call, brothers and sisters:
not many of you were wise
by human standards,
not many were powerful,
not many were of noble birth.
But God chose what is foolish
in the world to shame the wise;
God chose what is weak
in the world to shame the strong;
God chose what is low and despised
in the world, things that are not,
to reduce to nothing things that are,
so that no one might boast
in the presence of God.
He is the source of your life in Christ Jesus.

— 1Corinthians 1:26-30

Your Way

As I pray,
reveal to me
Your way
for me
to You,
Lord God.
Amen.

— **Br. John Mark Falkenhain, O.S.B. (2003)**

Prayer for Guidance in Choosing a Profession

GERMAN

Gott, seit meiner Geburt bist Du mein Begleiter. Du führst mich, auch wenn ich es mir nicht immer bewusst bin. Du hast mich erschaffen. Du kennst mich. Lass mich verstehen, welchen Weg Du für mein Leben vorgesehen hast. Hilf mir in dieser schwierigen Entscheidung der Berufswahl.

ENGLISH

God, since my birth you are my companion. You guide me even though I am not always aware of it. You created me. You know me. Let me understand what way you have foreseen for my life. Help me in this difficult decision of choosing a profession.

— **Br. Mauritius Honegger, O.S.B. (2007)**
Abbey of Einsiedeln, Switzerland

All My Ways

All my days
And all my ways
Are known to you, O Lord.

Help me know
My way to you
That I may love you, Lord.

— Novice Timothy Wymore, O.S.B.

My Choice

I chose a rather smallish world,
high on a smallish hill
where I could mill it day by day
to taste its mint and dill.

The biggish world has laughed a lot;
it thinks I chose too small,
but I have secret microscopes
that make my world grow tall.

Right past the birds and through the clouds
and higher than the sky
and deeper too till that be up—
I hardly have to try.

The fun of it has made me laugh
The monster bugs and flowers
that grow up big and fat and tall
and gobble up the hours.

The smallest bit that comes my way
I take into my eye
and find in it a simple food
to feed this hungry spy.

By seeing smaller I have grown
to be my very size—
the image of the unseen God
who makes me too to rise.

— **Fr. Harry Hagan, O.S.B. (1972)**

Beck and Call

Jesus, you have called me.
"Come to Me," you beckon my heart.
Well, here I am.

I desire to know you, to follow you.
Place me where you will
and set me to the task you've chosen
for my salvation and the good of others.

Answering your call,
I ask for all you desire of me.
Come, Lord Jesus.

— **Br. Francis de Sales Wagner, O.S.B. (2008)**

Return to the Lord Your God

CONVERSION/RECONCILIATION

*Rend your hearts
and not your clothing.
Return to the Lord, your God,
for he is gracious and merciful,
slow to anger,
and abounding in steadfast love,
and relents from punishing.*

— Joel 2:13

Reconciliation

As he, the Father of the wayward one,
   Awaited him with anxious, searching eye,
   And asked with hopeful heart all passers-by
   If they, perchance, had met his long-lost son;
And when he saw, as day was almost done,
   A weary, way-worn wanderer draw nigh,
   He hastened forth to greet with joyous cry
   His child—his cup of joy, full, overrun,
So now, the Spouse of Christ, His Holy Church,
   In sadness seeks her sinful, erring child,
   Who ventured far to gain earth's fleeting fame;
But when the sinner ends at last her search
   By coming humbly to be reconciled,
   His Mother's joy mounts high—a burning flame.

— Fr. Rupert Ostdick, O.S.B. (1944)

Prayer to Forgive

Merciful God, help me to forgive the wrong done to me,
to let go of old hurts: the unkind or presumptuous word,
the unfair demand, the impatience, the ingratitude,
the lack of support in time of need.

Seemingly long forgotten, these grievances flare up
occasionally, and I know I am being tempted
toward resentment and bitterness.
Help me to stamp out these flames
before they consume me,
to fight this fire with the fire of divine love.

Help me to recognize my own faults,
trusting in your mercy.
Then in gratitude, help me not only to forgive those
who harm me, but love them as you do this poor sinner.
Overcome us all by your love.
For however short we fall, we all fall short of you.
May none of us be lost.
Lift us up, Lord, and direct us according to your will.

— Br. Francis de Sales Wagner, O.S.B. (2008)

The City

Soul:

My heart is a city
Through which you ride
Like a caped crusader
You lay down your life
For the love of the city
You don your disguise
Fight the bad guys
For the love of the city

Christ:

Your heart is not open
These walls are high
I scale like a spider
I sneak and I slide
For the love of the city
I crawl in the night
Just to make right
Your heart the city

Soul:

The city is gloom
Begging for day
You come in the darkness

And break through the clay
For the love of the city
You bring in the bright
Your weapon is light
For the love of the city

— Fr. Christian Raab, O.S.B. (2005)

Help Along the Way

Merciful Father, thank you
for forgiving my sins.
Help me to imitate your love
by being a forgiving person.
May I see you in others,
not just in people I like
and get along with,
but also in the difficult ones.
You have given me the difficult ones
so that I have opportunities
to practice patience,
forgiveness, and love.
They are the people
who will help me get to heaven.

— **Fr. Joseph Cox, O.S.B. (1998)**

Take Up Your Cross and Follow Me

Christian Discipleship

Jesus called the crowd
with his disciples, and said to them,
"If any want to become my followers,
let them deny themselves
and take up their cross and follow me.
For those who want to save their life
will lose it, and those who lose their life
for my sake, and for the sake of the gospel,
will save it."

— Mark 8:34-35

Baptized in Christ

Baptized in Christ, we claim his cross,
the victory he won.
and dying we shall rise with him,
for we with Christ are one.

Baptized in Christ, we live his life:
God's will in us be done.
May we by all we do proclaim
the love that makes us one.

Baptized in Christ, we follow him,
and we with him shall run
until we match his every step
and so with Christ are one.

Baptized in Christ, we testify
the Kingdom has begun.
Christ sows and reaps throughout the world
and gathers us as one.

Baptized in Christ, we know his grace
that cannot be undone.
Its bounty spreads through all the earth
and leavens us as one.

Baptized in Christ, our dawn and day,
our noon and setting sun;
in him we bless all time and space,
for all in Christ are one.

Baptized in Christ we praise our God:
the Father and the Son
who with the Spirit live and reign,
Eternal Three in One.

— **Fr. Harry Hagan, O.S.B. (1972)**

Prayer to Do God's Will

God, free me of self
that I may walk
in *your* way.

— Br. Dominic Warnecke, O.S.B. (1961)

More Like You

Lord God, give me your mind
so that I may think as you think;
your ears to hear as you hear;
your eyes to see as you see;
your words to speak as you speak;
and your heart to feel as you feel.
May you make me more like you
so that I may be an instrument
of your love and grace. Amen.

— Br. Elijah Luckett, O.S.B. (2011)

Prayer for Gifts of the Holy Spirit

God our Creator,
give us the *spirit of wisdom*
to know that we are formed
in your image and likeness.

All Powerful Lord,
grant us the *spirit of fortitude*
to face the joys and challenges of the future.

God of the humble and poor,
bestow on us *the spirit of the fear of the Lord*
so that we might know your truth.

Merciful God,
bring us into the light of the
spirit of your counsel,
so that we may live abundantly in your love.

Transcendent God,
send forth *the spirit of piety* on us
so that we may worship you
with righteous hearts.

All Provident God,
shower on us *the spirit of knowledge*
so that we may discern your will.

Eternal and Loving Father,
deliver into our hearts and minds and
hands this day *the spirit of understanding,*
so that we might walk in harmony
with your Son, Jesus Christ,
who lives and reigns with you
and the Holy Spirit,
one God for ever and ever.

Amen.

— **Fr. Guerric DeBona, O.S.B. (1981)**

Loaf and Fish

They say there will be a shortage of us,
and the shortage will be shorter still.
Watch out, they say, lest you be eaten alive,
but who has time to watch out,
so much there is to do,
so many to be fed, and we so short on food:
five barley loaves and two fish,
little enough for the growing hungry crowd.
Surely they will eat us too.

Nothing to do but let this Jesus feed the many.
He did it once or twice a while ago
so many with so little with more to spare—
yes, this Jesus knows how to—
to feed too many with too little so full
and we, we need only be the loaf and fish
as was this Jesus too.

Yes, be loaf, be fish!

Be vitamin enriched wonder bread,
but not all white, be brown bread too,
whole wheat, full kernel taken altogether
with bran to push, and hardy dark pumpernickel
as black as it is good for you,

and maybe for a change, some days, rye
just to humor the crowd.

And for a fish you can choose rainbow trout
or big mouth bass, which I recommend to some,
catfish or blue gill, but not goldfish.
Still whatever you will,
but be fish too, like this Jesus,
swim and breathe water and be caught for food
to feed the many full.

Yes, be loaf and fish for food,
For if this Jesus feeds you to them,
when they gather you up,
you will be more than when you began.

— **Fr. Harry Hagan, O.S.B. (1972)**

One for the Breaking

(Inspired by George Bernanos' The Dialogues of the Carmelites)

I'm afraid
Death comes to the nation
I abstain from humiliation
I'd be alone
Than go through this suffering
I can't see what good it do
I can't see the light

I refrain afraid of this calling
What good is pain?
What good is falling?
I'll be the one to carry on living
I can't see what good it do
To let go of life

You make haste
You answer this calling
They don't know your names
They don't see you falling
Will you be with them?
With them in the rising?
I can't see what good it do
Can you save their lives?

Will the body be

One for the breaking
One forsaken
One in desolation
So that they may see?

Will the body be
One for the nations
One in celebration
One for the breaking
So that they believe?

Will the body be one?

I'm afraid
Afraid of the slaughter
This is the cost
To recover our daughter
Will our innocence spend
Like cash for the others?
Do I offer my blood and tears
My weakness this night?

Will I remain,
Remain in the shelter?
Missing a member
They head to the altar
Don't leave them alone
To face their pursuers

To offer their love and pleas
To take the knife

May the body be
One for the breaking
One forsaken
One in desolation
So that they may see

May the body be
One for the nations
One in celebration
One for the breaking
So that they believe

May the body be one

I'm late
I'm late for my station
I'll stand in line for elimination
I pray for strength
I pray for the gumption
I see what good we do
When we join our lives

We're on stage
On stage for the nation
We stand in line

To give our oration
We pay for sins
by duty not reason
They'll see what good we do
One day when they try

Pyres are lit
muskets are loaded
Blades are raised
Heads in a bucket
On this very ground
Where our blood is spilling
New trees are growing
Water is flowing

Let the body be
One for the breaking
One forsaken
One in desolation
So that they may see

One for the nations
One in celebration
One for the breaking
So that they believe

Let the body be one
> — Fr. Christian Raab, O.S.B. (2005)

God Is the Way

God, Creator of us all,
Yours is the day and yours is the night.
Be our defense in times of trial;
Be our strength in times of loss.
May your Son be our joy and our light;
May He be our Life on the way.
Amen.

— Fr. Cyprian Davis, O.S.B. (1951)

Have Mercy, Son of David!

(based on Mark 10:46-52)

Have mercy, Son of David!
By mercy set us free.
Have mercy, Son of David!
O Lord, that we may see.
For we, like Bartimeus,
cry out with heart and soul.
We ask for faith to follow,
for faith to make us whole.

Have mercy, Son of David!
Give us your eyes to see
that we may see the Kingdom
in its simplicity.
May we behold the glory,
the majesty and grace
of your mysterious beauty,
alive in every face.

— Fr. Harry Hagan, O.S.B. (1972)

Seek and Strive After Peace

Looking for God Amid Struggle

Rejoice in the Lord always;
again I will say, Rejoice.
Let your gentleness be known to everyone.
The Lord is near.
Do not worry about anything,
but in everything by prayer
and supplication with thanksgiving
let your requests be made known to God.
And the peace of God,
which surpasses all understanding,
will guard your hearts
and your minds in Christ Jesus.

— Philippians 4:4-7

God's Grace Provides

Successes and joys
projects complete
plans carried out
things gone right
blessings abound—
God's grace provides.

Life's disappointments
dreams unfulfilled
hopes unrealized
chaos of feelings
aching hearts—
God's grace provides.

Questions arise
doubt hovers near
strength subsides
resolve grows weak
the going gets tough—
God's grace provides.

Family and friends
soul-mates, sisters and brothers
all for a time
length of days varies

but lasting forever—
God's grace provides.

Do not be afraid
walk through the darkness
sail through the storm
travel on in hope
move forward in faith—
God's grace provides.

Yesterdays of memory
tomorrows of imagining
have been and yet will be
todays lived now
all will be well—
God's grace provides.

— **Fr. Julian Peters, O.S.B. (1983)**

Comfort

Comfort your people, Lord
Comfort them.

Their hearts are heavy
Their cares many,
As they bear the burden of the day.

Comfort your people, Lord,
Comfort them.

Heal the sick,
Ease the pain of those preparing to die.
Comfort the sorrowing.
Show them your way.

Soften the hearts of those
Who make strife all the day long.
So that they may enjoy your peace,
And give you glory all the day.

Comfort your people, Lord,
Comfort them.

Ready their hearts,
Prepare them to do your will,
So that they may walk in your truth.
Guide their hearts to fear your name.

Liken them to the tree
Planted by flowing waters,
So that all they do shall prosper,
As they ponder your law day and night.

Comfort your people, Lord,
Comfort them.

Lift up their hearts,
Lift them out of the darkness
Of selfishness and sin
Into your own saving light.

Lead them to your holy mountain,
To the place where you dwell,
So that they may be free from sin,
And praise your name all the day.

Comfort your people, Lord,
Comfort them.

Their hearts are heavy,
Their cares many,
As they bear the burden of the day.

Comfort your people, Lord,
Comfort them.

— **Fr. Simeon Daly, O.S.B. (1944)**

Where are You, God?

My God, my God, why have you deserted me?
You make so as to lead me
Through pastures to still waters
There is nothing I shall want, you say.

A table is before me
My cup overflows with wine
There is nothing I lack: it's almost true
Everything is mine but you.

Be with me, Lord
The earth is yours, and all it holds
And those who live there too
So where are you?

Be with me, Lord
For I know you are there
Grant me faith like a mustard seed
For I am deaf and blind.

Too much noise, God
Too many thoughts and lights
and fights and books
To be with you, Lord
Grant me pastures and still waters.

That in your silence I may hear you
That in your darkness I may see you
That my mustard seed die and rise
And your servant know your table true.

— **Novice Timothy Wymore, O.S.B.**

Secure My spirit

Awake my soul, O Lord.
Gently, O Lord, rouse my spirit,
open my eyes and chase away the darkness.
Scatter all my anxiety so that I may hide in you.

Shield me from distraction,
unease and doubt,
from all that threatens to harm me
or separate me from you.

Show me your face this day.
Look upon me, and pierce my inner being
with your unfailing light.
Conquer all that divides me,
and center all my affections on your love alone.

Invigorate me, enliven my spirit,
uplift my mind and lighten my step.
You are at the center of my entire being.
Shower me with your grace
so I may be radiant in your presence.

Preserve me in peace
so it may flow into and feed
my prayer, my work and my union

with all your creation.
Strengthen me in your service
and shelter me from all sin
so that your will alone is my sentry.

Awake my soul,
surrender my heart,
and secure my spirit, O Lord.

— Br. Francis de Sales Wagner, O.S.B. (2008)

Mysteries Unfolding

Shadows at the foot of the Cross
cold darkness of the tomb—
dispelled into light
and warmed into life
by the bright dawn of Eternity

Events of long ago
played out in present time;
in seasons of grace

and every moment of our lives.

His dying and rising
Our letting go and taking hold

Momentary pain
Enduring hope
Lasting peace

— **Fr. Julian Peters, O.S.B. (1983)**

Take All

Take what is broken, Lord,
And make us mended;
Take what is tired,
And make us renewed;
Take what is scattered,
And make us whole.
And that which is lost,
Make us truly found.
Amen.

— Fr. Cyprian Davis, O.S.B. (1951)

Human Heart

My heart—
a battleground
where only one fights
but still loses.
To be captured
is my desire.
Why fight Him, then,
who is not your enemy?

— **Br. John Mark Falkenhain, O.S.B. (2003)**

Hold Fast to Mystery

Resting in God Alone

Devote yourselves to prayer,
keeping alert in it with thanksgiving.
At the same time pray for us as well,
that God will open to us a door
for the word, that we may declare
the mystery of Christ.

— Colossians 4:2-3

Prayer Before Worship

Blessed are you, Lord God, Creator of the Universe.
    You give breath to all that lives
    and fill us with your Spirit
    that we may serve one another.
We have gathered here
    in the name of our Lord, Jesus Christ.
He is in our midst now—make us worthy ministers
    that we may bring him present for all your people.
You, Creator God, are the giver of all gifts,
    and among us you have spread a richness
    that reveals your generosity.
        May those blessed with the gift of music
          lead our song in harmony
          with the praise of all creation.
        May those called to proclaim your word
          read with clarity and power
          for the glory of your name.
        May those who minister the Body
          and Blood of Christ prompt others
          to recognize that we are all
          part of the mystery we celebrate.
        May we who have been chosen
          for the order of presbyters
          prayerfully lead the worship
          of the whole assembly.

Loving God, bless all who participate
    in praising your goodness.
We know we are unable to fully recognize
    all you are and have given us,
    but we are confident that our desire
    to praise you is pleasing in your sight.
Be with us now as we strive to serve
    the sisters and brothers you have given us here.
May God Almighty, Father, Son, and + Holy Spirit
    be with us, now and always, and forever and ever.
Amen.

— **Fr. Bede Cisco, O.S.B. (1974)**

Thank You, Lord

Thank you, Lord,
for everything I do not see:
for wires and pipes
that hide within the walls,
for those who put them there
so long ago to serve.
And thank you too
for people passing by
who nod or smile,
but, I regret to say,
escape me unaware.
For every unseen hand
that washes, cooks or cleans
and every single kindness
so simply offered
that it passes me without a word
to mark its wide humanity.
For my oblivious culpability
I honestly ask some pardon
and give this thanks again
for everything I do not see.

— **Fr. Harry Hagan, O.S.B. (1972)**

On the Way to Damascus

My Lord and my God,
I lived so long without you;
I know that lonely road.

You knew me,
but I did not know you,
until I met you on the way.

Keep my sight, I care not.
For I have heard far greater things.

Meeting you was like hearing a song,
which I knew I'd never heard,
but which somehow I already knew by heart.
I felt like I had always known it,
but had given up on ever hearing it.

And now that I have heard it,
now that I have met you, my Lord,
I pray that the song
never leave my head
nor my heart.

— **Fr. Paul Nord, O.S.B. (2003)**

Food for the Journey

Lord God, the Eternal Source of all being,

My soul hungers for you because you have sown
your Word in my heart.
So often, though, I lose my way
because I am distracted, preoccupied,
even focused on good things for the wrong reasons.
My vision becomes clouded,
and I feed on things that ultimately leave me empty.

Lead me by your Spirit into the desert of my soul,
the secret room of my heart, where you invite me
to a personal relationship with Jesus, your Son.
Help me to encounter and embrace there
what I truly desire,
and what you truly wish to give me,
in union with your church throughout the world.

Deepen my prayer through your grace
so that I may listen and hear
your loving invitation,
your gentle call.
Help me to recognize and respond
to your ever-present voice
through the surrender of whatever
holds me back or turns me away.

May I discover—and rediscover each day—
your creating power, your saving grace,
your constant presence.
I wish to taste and see that you are good.
Fill me with your wisdom, your food
for the journey toward you.

Bring my heart into prayer,
so that my whole time and being
rest in you and you alone,
that I may bear the fruit that your food alone provides.
Lord of the harvest, feed me.

— Br. Francis de Sales Wagner, O.S.B. (2008)

Observe the Rests

No musician would attempt to play or sing a piece of metered music without first checking the key signature and timing. To honor the composer's wishes, we should respect the directions that are given by such indicators. To accidentally or even purposely ignore a rest can be disruptive and disrespectful. We can compensate, but it certainly does not indicate reverence either for the composer or for ourselves.

O God, our Creator, you have composed a marvelous piece of art in each of us, and it should be out of respect for you that we observe the indications for rest that you have laid out in our lives. We sometimes ignore or play through those times, and in so doing we make your composition less beautiful, and it becomes more our own work than your art. Grant us, we pray, the wisdom to *observe the rests!*

— **Fr. Jeremy King, O.S.B. (1971)**

The Heavens by Your Word

The heavens by your Word were made:
some billion galaxies,
whose fiery mass times light by light
explodes as energy.
When first you spoke, you struck the spark
that loosed this majesty:
a billion, billion racing stars
against the dark set free.

Orion's sword, Magellan's cloud,
the Milky Way in flight,
Andromeda's majestic swirl,
black holes, and bending light.
The planets held by gravity
move round our little sun
while all the universe expands
with time and space as one.

Lord, what are we that we can probe
the mystery of your ways?
And what shall we return to you
except this simple praise?
What vastness shall compare with you?
O True Infinity!
What height or depth shall measure you?
Most Blessed Trinity!

— **Fr. Harry Hagan, O.S.B. (1972)**

Prayer During a Blizzard

(January 1978)

O God,
of old you spoke to our father Noah
and told him to prepare an ark to save
    your faithful people,
    together with the birds and animals
    of your creation.
You drew your people to yourself,
    sparing Noah and your friends
    and the creatures your hand had made.
Then you renewed your covenant,
    promising never again to interrupt
    the order you had established.
Now, amidst the sinfulness of our world
    today you rain down snow upon the earth
    to cover your creation
    with your goodness.
Through your action in our lives
    you remind us you are ever-present,
    always renewing the covenant
    you gave to our ancestors.
You bring us closer to one another and to you
    by slowing down our lives,
    confounding our projects and plans,
    and giving us your holy rest.

We thank you for bringing us together,
>to share at your table
>and in your life-giving presence.
To you be all glory and honor,
>praise and thanksgiving,
>now and forever.
Amen.

— **Fr. Bede Cisco, O.S.B. (1974)**

Know the Power of Christ's Resurrection

Lent/Easter

*I want to know Christ
and the power of his resurrection
and the sharing of his sufferings
by becoming like him in his death,
if somehow I may attain
the resurrection from the dead.
I press on to make the goal my own,
because Christ Jesus has made me his own.*

— Philippians 3:10-12

Passion: A Lenten Prayer

God our Father,

Your Son, taking on our humanity,
was led by your Spirit into the desert
to confront the passions
that threaten to mislead us all.
In the garden, he willingly accepted the agony
of knowing what it is to be cut off from God
when we follow those passions.
And on the cross,
he became sin itself
to release us from its grip.

Descending into the depths of hell,
he showed us how to confront
and accept our humanity
so that we may rise with him in Easter glory,
take on his divinity, and ascend
to you in Spirit and truth.

During this Lenten season
of heightened prayer, fasting, and almsgiving,
help us to enter into the true Passion of Christ
to confront and overcome the human passions
that threaten to delude us into self-exaltation.

Grant us the humility that allows us
to be more human, more like Christ
—who humbled himself for us.
May we know the joy of descending
the ladder of humility with him,
so that we may ascend to you
with him through self-knowledge.

Increase our faith, hope, and love,
so that through self-sacrifice
we may seek the things that are above
while keeping our feet firmly planted
on the ground from which we were formed
by you, the Creator who gives us all
that is good, and promises
more than we can imagine.

Through the same Christ, our Lord. Amen.

— **Br. Francis de Sales Wagner, O.S.B. (2008)**

This Great Week, This Holy Week

Memories
vague and vivid
like videos and DVDs of our past

Triggered by sight, smell, sound

Most often mental activity

But when memory comes into action
when mental activity is joined
to forms and figures
motion and song

When mind, heart and soul
are synchronized
with the movements of the body

We have ritual.

We come now to the threshold
of a Great Week,
a Holy Week—
a course of days
when the stories of our salvation are told again
when sacred memories are played out once more

in solemn chant and stately movement—
with sights and sounds and smells
body, mind and spirit
caught up in wonder and awe.

Let us lay aside all apprehension
abandoning ourselves to what lies ahead
to the power of ritual
juxtaposing memory and action
the familiar and comfortable
the different and even the strange.

There was once
a triumphal entry into Jerusalem, the Holy City
One riding on the colt of an ass
songs and acclamations
the waving of branches
and strewing of garments in the way
to greet the Son of David.

Now amid solemn Hosannas
we, too, go up to the Holy City
in garments all red and crimson
with branches carried in stately array
bells and banners
chimes and voices—

And we cross the threshold
of this Great Week
this Holy Week.

In the morning
after chimes are stilled
and acclamations silenced
begins the gentle wail of Lamentations
calling into the present
the sorrows of the past
and the promise of the future.

We go up to the Altar of God
to behold the Lamb of God
slain for us.

Recalling the story in solemn form—
shouting crowds
confessions of faith
and confused denials
trial and torture
the uphill climb
gently laid away in a tomb.

Do this in memory of Me
as you pass over the threshold
of this Great Week
this Holy Week.

Go about the city
spending time in prayer
then to make ready
the upper room
of our hearts
a place sent apart—
to engage the ancient memory
the deliverance of generations long past.

See how
with splendor laid aside
where charity and love prevail
in washing and being washed
God is surely found.

Take and eat
be nourished and fed
sustained and strengthened—
cherish this sweet moment
for soon come betrayal and trial.

Take this
do this
in memory of Me
as you move through
this Great Week
this Holy Week.

Away to a garden
not of paradise now
but of sweat and tears
a garden dark
of lonely repose.

Move through the streets
no more with gladness and singing
from palace to court
bound and beaten
forgotten, forsaken
as prophets foretold
the story unfolds.

Behold now the tree
not of glorious branches
but of naked wood
to the eye a tree of death
but for the soul a throne of glory.

Approach
bow and bend low
because by this Holy Cross
He has redeemed the world.

Fall prostrate in prayer
listen and wait
for the journey is not yet complete
through this Great Week
this Holy Week.
Great silence reigns on earth
life has died
death lives.

Do not take, do not eat
but wait in fasting—
dark descends
but dawn approaches.

See the fire brighten the night
behold the pillar of light moving forward.

Hear the stories
of that happy fault
of the generations' journey
promises made
water in the wilderness
life to dry bones
hunger satisfied
waiting rewarded.

Come to the water
and remember your birth.
Take up the light
to illumine your way.
Feast on this food
and live again.
Dawn has shattered the darkness
glory fills you

Jesus Christ is risen!
Once more remembered
again believed
renewed, refreshed
reborn
through the power of
this Great Week
this Holy Week.

— **Fr. Julian Peters, O.S.B. (1983)**

Looking to the Cross: A Lenten Prayer

Almighty Father, rich in love
and generous in mercy,
as we prepare ourselves to receive
your ultimate gift of love,
we ask you to bless our prayer,
work, and almsgiving
during these 40 days of Lent.
Teach us the art of humility;
help us to see
ourselves
as you see us.

Guide all of us to show love
to those who are difficult to love
and mercy to those who need our mercy.
As we open our hearts to others,
may they be filled with wonder
and awe as we look to the cross
and your triumph
over sin and death,
and anticipate your second coming.
Amen.

— Br. Luke Waugh, O.S.B. (2010)

If It Dies, It Bears Much Fruit

To everyone who conquers,
I will give permission
to eat from the tree of life
that is in the paradise of God.
— Rev. 2:7

A lifeless body in a tomb.

Alone.

Defeated.

Wrapped in burial cloths
of misery, fear, and failure.

A decaying grain concealed in darkest land.

Mystery awaits the morn.

Thin light spreads over a horizon unaware
of what the earth cannot contain.

The soil is soaked with divinity's dew.

The seed of humanity sheds its rotten garments.

The wound within opens.

A tender shoot appears.

It emerges above the soil.

Pulled toward the rising sun,
it is green, full of sap.

Roots crack through and discard
the seed's hard but fragile casing…

… surge through and clutch the earth…

… drink from the brimming river.

The stalk grows thicker, taller.

Stems become branches.

Buds blossom and leaves unfurl.

Within them the birds of heaven sing their song.

Hanging there is ripened fruit.

Good for food.

Pleasing to the eye.

Desirable for gaining wisdom.

Fruit better than gold.

A woman enters the land.

She seeks a burial plot, and finds the tree.

She is amazed at what has arisen there.

Taking some of the fruit, she eats.

Urged by an angel, she shares it.

Naked again, eyes are opened.

Wrapped in the light of faith, hope, love.

Triumphant.

Together.

A vibrant body in a garden.

Planted in the house of the Lord.

Still bearing fruit when they are old.

Surrounding the Tree of Life.
Singing *Alleluia!*

— **Br. Francis de Sales Wagner, O.S.B. (2008)**

The Lord Gives You This Sign

Advent/Christmas

All this took place
to fulfill what had been spoken
by the Lord through the prophet:
"Look, the virgin shall conceive and bear a son,
and they shall name him Emmanuel,"
which means, "God is with us."

— Matthew 1:22-23

Visitation

Two women meet,
cousins yet more than kin—
bound now to one another
by pregnant surprise.

Their unpredictable God has laughed at nature
and made the childless and the virgin bear.
She of the leaping womb, thought barren,
bears the restlessness of her God.

And the virgin unknown
becomes the magnifying glass
that makes great her God for all to see.

The women embrace:
forgotten hope surprised by life
embraces surpassing love.

Meeting they touch
the old and the new
the forgotten and the unknown
now revealed in mystery
as ancient desire and time's fullness.

The simple majesty
of their common meeting

is remembered as the uncommon visitation
of God come among us.
Shall our own forgotten hope
protect us from surprise?

Perhaps!

Shall our fear of being known
cause us to turn and hide
from this—God's embrace?

It is possible.

Shall we trade
the restlessness of God
for oblivion?

Also possible.

But these women,
Elizabeth and Mary,
desire and fullness,
call us to laugh with our unpredictable God
who comes to visit
such a warm and generous embrace
upon our quaking hearts.

— **Fr. Harry Hagan, O.S.B. (1972)**

Emmanuel

By extending to all

Careful rest,
Harmonic stillness,
Radiant modesty,
Intelligent wonder,
Selfless delight,
Tender strength,

we are first embraced
by the One
whose tiny arms
extend beyond
and over all.

— Br. Francis de Sales Wagner, O.S.B. (2008)

Epilogue

Give Me This Water

Jesus cried out,
"Let anyone who is thirsty come to me,
and let the one who believes in me drink.
As the scripture has said,
'Out of the believer's heart
shall flow rivers of living water.'"

— **John 7:37-38**

Give Me This Water

(Meditation on Jesus and the Samaritan woman at the well, John 4:5-42)

"I thirst," Jesus said from the cross (John 19:28).
The Son of God longs for our faith in him,
our conversion, our eternal union in the Holy Trinity.
And to prove it, as St. Paul says, he died for us
while we were still sinners.

For this reason, Jesus says to the Samaritan woman—
a foreigner in a hostile region, and a sinner—"Give me a
drink." She has come to the deep, dark well to draw stagnant
water because it's all she knows. Yet, hidden in her heart is a
thirst for something more life-giving, and Jesus patiently
draws that holy desire out of her. He slowly and lovingly
turns her toward conversion by offering her "living water."

However, the Gospel passage is not about water, but rather
life in Spirit and truth that Jesus offers to us all. Later in
John's Gospel, Jesus extends this invitation: "Let anyone
who thirsts come to me and drink. Whoever believes in me,
as scripture says: 'Rivers of living water will flow
from within him'" (John 7:37-38).

Without water for our bodies, we die. And without the
living water of the Spirit, our souls remain submerged in
the Samaritan woman's deep, dark well of lifeless water.

However, Jesus does not force our hand. He engages the woman on her terms. He allows her to direct the flow of the conversation.

Gradually, she begins to trust him, and finally says to him, "Give me this water." The moment for her conversion has arrived, but Jesus does not condemn. Again, he slowly and lovingly states the facts, and then allows her to absorb and respond to them at her own pace.

The Samaritan woman prefigures the Church.
Just as Isaac, Jacob, and Moses meet their wives at a well,
Christ engages his Bride
(the Church, and our individual souls),
and offers us his life-giving Spirit.

Just as with the Samaritan woman, Jesus is patient and loving with us. His hope is that finally, like her, we will believe, leave behind our old water jar (way of life), and pick up a new vessel that pours his Spirit into the lives of others.

He alone satisfies our thirst for eternal life.
Let us ask him, "Give me this water."

— **Br. Francis de Sales Wagner, O.S.B. (2008)**